Elijah's Book of Poems

Keep Knowledge Flowing

By   Elijah Latin

Table of contents

Acknowledgement

Introduction

Acknowledgements

I want to thank God for giving me the inspiration to
write this book of poems. A special thanks to my wife
Debra, sons Wesley and Major for their support.
Also, in memory of my mother, mother in-law, and
father in-law who always supported me.
I want to thank my Church family and my Pastor.
Thanks to all the staff at Amazon and KDP, thank
you one and all. Also, a special thanks to all my friends
and neighbors in Korhville, Texas.
Thanks, everyone.   Elijah Latin

Long live the King, King Jesus.

Introduction

Its good when a person, being the author, can write about things and beings, then become that thing or that person who he or she is writing about. We all have a poem inside of us. We are inspired to speak out with words on paper, that others might enjoy what we have stored up on the inside. Some of what Elijah has is Spiritual and inspirational, with plenty of love. There is the humorous side that helps bring some joy and laughter to a sad countenance. The author gives voice to the trees and the animals. He speaks for beings and things alike. Elijah puts himself in his subject's stead. The book is inspiring. The book is full of joyful, spiritual and humorous poems. The poems are written from the great imagination of the author, through inspirations of the heart and from some life experiences. Enjoy and thanks for your support.

Chapter 1

Spiritual & Inspirational

If You Love Me (God)

If you love Me, no hill or Mountain is too steep,
If you love Me, feed My sheep.

If you love Me, you'll love My Holy way of life,
You'll love your husband you'll love your wife.'

If you love Me, on your child you wouldn't spare the rod,
You will let them know that I'm The Living God.

If you love Me, you will love one another,
You will obey your father and mother.

If you love Me, you will turn from your wicked ways,
You would seek Me in your youthful days.

If you love Me, you wouldn't be a tale bearer or backbiter,
You would cling to Me a lot tighter.

If you love Me, you would visit the shut in and the sick,
You won't walk around being slick.

If you love Me, you'll love your enemy and not hate,
If one is hungry, you'll share your plate.

If you love Me, you'll pray and walk together as one,
In Heaven, liars and sinners there are none.

If you love Me, you'll always help those that are in need,
Love will show up in your deed.

The Strait Gate

The Infallible Word of God is Heaven sent,
Of your sins you must repent.

There'll be no going around or climbing over the wall,
If you think so you're in for a fall.

The way is narrow, and the road is strait,
You must enter through this gate.

While on earth if by God's fire you've not been tried,
Your access to Heaven will be denied.

There's no escaping from the depths of the fiery pit,
If sinning ways you don't quit.

The Word came down to earth as a ransom for many,
Sinners in Heaven there aren't any.

To get through the gate you must become a new man,
There's no altering God's plan.

There's a way that might seem right unto you,
However, with God it'll never do.

When the road is gone and the Angels shuts the gate,
For them that are left it will be too late.

The Bible tells us to keep watch, pray and be ready,
Follow the Word strait and steady.

The Lord's Way, Man's Way

The Lord will never lead you down the wrong way,
Man will lead you astray.
The Lord will see to it that His people have bread,
Depending on man you'll end up dead.

The Lord will forgive and throw it away into the sea,
Man will never let it be.
The Lord will come and wipe away all your tears,
Man will abuse you for years.

The Lord will always be there as your best friend,
To get what he wants, man will pretend.
The Lord is kind and wins people with gentle love,
Man will squeeze you like a glove.

For friends the Lord volunteered to lay down His life and die,
To save his life, man will lie.
The Lord wants us to do things for His Glory,
Man will tell his own story.

The Lord sends a messenger with glad tidings to be heard,
Man will try to twist the Word.
The Lord said for a husband to love his wife,
Man will ruin and take her life.

The Lord will do nothing before its appointed time,
Man won't wait, he'll commit a crime.
Man often, separates us by color or race,
The Lord accepts us all in one place.

Please Forgive Me O' Lord

Please forgive me O' Lord for the way I've treated your Son,
Now that I know just what I've done.

Please forgive me O' Lord for listening to the gossip I heard,
For not hearing and obeying your Word.

Please forgive me O' Lord for all the wrong things I have did,
For being disobedient when I was a kid.

Please forgive me O' Lord for slothfully chastising my son,
For walking around like a loaded gun.

Please forgive me O' Lord for taking your name in vain,
For causing other people undeserved pain.

Please forgive me O' Lord for the times my friends came by,
For making my children tell them a lie.

Please forgive me O' Lord for not doing as I was told,
I'm striving to be Holy and bold.

Please forgive me O' Lord for being slow answering your call,
I'm striving to be like Apostle Paul.

Please forgive me O' Lord for not thanking you for every day,
For trying to do things my own way.

Please forgive me O' Lord, for leaving the Church in the cold,
Thank You Lord for taking me back into the fold.

The Rewards of Obedient Suffering

Jesus was born because of man's sin,
Among animals in a manger outside an
Inn.

Tiding spread by keepers of flock,
Something King Herod couldn't
block.

As a Child He obeyed His mother,
Never heard of Him fighting His
brother.

Baptized by a prophet named John,
Being in the scripture it had to be
done.

He healed the sick and raised the dead,
Caused a man with palsy to take up
his bed.

Not being one who just sit and talked,
Because of His power lame men
walked.

For our sins the cross He did bear,
Between two sinners they hung
Him there.

Love for us caused the Lord much pain,
He died that life we would gain.

God

For His pleasure from the earth man was created,
With a woman he was mated.

In the Garden of Eden God gave man a job to do,
An evil serpent was there too.

By the evil serpent the woman was deceived,
Of his job man was relieved.

God told them to go be fruitful and multiply,
Because of sin man is born to die.

God loved man enough to keep him around,
Now man must till the ground.

God said in His Word if a man doesn't work, he does not eat,
God's Word we cannot beat.

The earth and its fullness all belong to God,
His yolk is easy man makes it hard.

God sent His only begotten Son as a ransom for many,
Others worthy there was not any.

While living here on earth if you want a long stay,
You must walk in God's way.

God loves a willing worker and a cheerful giver,
Whatever God promised He'll deliver.

Bearing the Cross

We all saw what happened to the green tree,
What'll happen to you and me?
If you want to follow Jesus there is a price,
Things will happen that aren't nice.

If they lied on Jesus no matter what you do,
You'll be lied on too.
A lot of people didn't want to believe Him,
You'll meet some like them.

If you don't fight people will call you weak,
You must turn the other cheek.
You must always treat your neighbor right,
Even if he knocks late at night.

With the needy you must share your bread,
Letting the seed of love spread.
If an enemy thirst you must give him a drink,
No matter what you think.

Walking in God's statue you must forgive,
If it's Holy you want to live.
There are certain conditions you must meet,
If you want Jesus to rest your feet.

Jesus is returning but we don't know the hour,
Bringing with Him great power.
If we don't want our life to be a total loss,
We must bear our own cross.

The New Man

We are often hearing people say they have changed,
From when they used to be deranged.
People are saying that they are saved and sanctified,
The old man in them have died.

If they changed on the inside and it's not just idle talk,
It'll should show up in their walk.
Moses met God and came back with a different look,
Its written in the Book.

People may be able to dress up the outside appearance,
But with God they have no clearance.
What a person has in them that they're trying to hide,
It'll show up on the outside.

If I confess that I met the Lord and have been born again,
Then I have become a new man.
The Lord will be the center and the head of my life,
My heart will have been under the knife.

I will have done like the pea and came out of my pod,
Caring for the things of God.
For Jesus I will go everywhere and be a bold witness,
Being equipped with Holy Ghost fitness.

Every day I will not fail to call upon the Lord's name,
In Him there is no shame.
Your heart will always reach out to help the needy,
For money you won't be greedy.

If indeed you are confessing to be a born-again Saint,
The Lord's blood you'll not taint.
With the old man cast out you've become a new creature,
In your life there is a new feature. (Jesus)

God Being Himself

The world had grown evil something had to be done,
To send someone worthy there was none.
There's a saying about having to do things yourself,
God's Word wasn't meant to collect dust on a shelf.

He came down in the foundation of the Holy Word,
Making sure of firsthand that it would be heard.
In the womb of a virgin a Temple for Him was formed,
Sent a message to her husband not to be alarmed.

Knowing all thoughts and every word that men would say,
Is the reason He came that way.
Out of the womb in the Temple His spirit dwelled within,
Being Holy in Him there was no sin.

Of every man, He knew what was hidden in his heart,
Those He touched the devil had to depart.
There were those who thought they could trap Him,
He was always ready for them.

When He got the news about His friend Lazarus being dead,
He didn't quit working He kept moving ahead.
After four days He came and He heard their cries,
He raised Lazarus up and dried their eyes.

Every day the Pharisees and Scribes He would always offend,
Of their evil ways they wouldn't mend.
He didn't come down to destroy but to fulfill the law,
In His Commandments there's no flaw.

He came down to earth and walked through all the land,
The whole world's in His hand.
Being formed by God in His own image we're His treasure,
We were made for His Pleasure.

Because He is not a man that He would tell a lie,
He has a spirit that'll never die.
Having Mercy, compassion and love He made a sacrifice,
For us He paid the ultimate price.

As He walked the earth, He told people about a place,
To get there you must seek His face.
He said that we must repent of our sins and be born again,
You can't get there being an unjust man.

He came down that He might show us the way we must go,
His voice His people will know.
With their eyes closed and mind shut up as being in a pod,
Had they looked they would've seen God.

He laid down His life and put old man death in its place,
When Jesus rose, He showed us His Grace.
With all power in His hand for Him nothing is too hard,
Because He's the Living God.

My Sheep

My sheep hear and know my voice,
They follow me by choice.

My sheep do not need to be peppered,
I am the good Shepherd.

I'm not one who says I'll do and then don't,
My sheep shall not want.

Although my sheep are sometime fasters,
They lay down in green pastures.

My sheep are led beside still water,
Love is their charter.

My sheep's days are never bored,
Their lives are restored.

I lead them down the path of righteousness,
My sheep will I bless.

The hills and the mountains may seem steep,
But I'm always with my sheep.

In all you do, put the Good Shepherd first,
Drink of My cup you'll never thirst.

Goodness and Mercy shall follow you all your days,
Walking in the Good Shepherd's ways.

A Pastor

The job that was given to him is very demanding,
He must have a good understanding.
As a Shepherd taking care of the Lord's herd,
He feeds the flock with God's Word.

Of the congregation, their burdens he'll bear,
With open arms he's always there.
Other preachers before him came and went away,
But he came prepared to stay.

When he gets happy his spirit will begin to shout,
His happy feet are dancing about.
Boldly following the straight and narrow path,
He strives to give a spiritual bath.

Men have come to him in friendship and in disguise,
The Lord has made him very wise.
People will talk about and they'll lie on him,
With a smile he forgives them.

He is a preacher, teacher, a friend and family man,
Working to carry out God's plan.
He stands praying for the people in a long prayer line,
Being drained he'll not whine.

Because of the love of Jesus and God's good Grace,
He is equipped to run the race.
All over the earth he is admired and loved by many,
From his people he won't steal a penny.

Do everything you can for your pastor while he yet live,
One day you won't be able to give.
Although God appointed him to watch over you,
Remember that he's human too.

He was appointed by the Lord to watch over the flock,
God has him working on a special clock.
In a good pastor revenge and hate you'll find none,
Of him it'll be said, "well done".

Love Knows

Love knows when to tell a child no,
Love knows when to let go.

Love knows when to stand and be bold,
Love is never rude or cold.

Love is true and given from a pure heart,
Love will not fall apart.

Love overcomes and conquers many things,
Love comes without strings.

Love will strive to keep the peace,
Love knows when to cease.

Love knows one is born to die,
Love knows when to cry.

Love will always have room to forgive,
Love knows the way to live.

Love knows, being in the hand of God there is no danger,
Love will help a needy stranger

Love will keep a secret for a friend,
Love will never end.

Love will stretch and love will bend,
Love knows how to mend.

The Presence of Evil

Whenever good thoughts enter my mind,
Evil thoughts are not far behind.

I must discern and choose that which is right,
Although evil puts up a fight.

Good will show me the outcome of the matter,
While evil hides the latter.

Evil tries hard to carry me to the pits,
Good intercedes giving me wits.

Although things are not always as they seem,
Evil lurks even in my dream.

Evil will make a bad thing look very nice,
Good cautions me to think twice.

Evil comes to kill steal and destroy,
Good comes to bring me joy.

Between good and evil there's a great race,
There's no second or third place.

Be mindful that evil will soon be put away,
Only good is here to stay.

Up on A High Pedestal

With an abode that reflects of a King's castle,
Dare to look out upon life's daily hassle.
Riding in the excessiveness of money's gain,
Passing deprived natives walking in pain.

Belittling the have-nots from a safe high perch,
Sitting in a seat of reign in the core of Church,
Feasting without cease while one who is lacking, fast.
Unable to see the image of your cast.

Unbroken errors to whom nil is never right,
Gamely poised to enter a fiery fight,
Constant cause of ado with revile of power.
Pouncing on one who is in a pose of cower.

Never once having shed no not even one tear,
For the unknown child who lives in fear.
Only for rebel flesh which causes much sighing,
Grieves your heart and keeps you crying.

There is one above, eyes looking down on all,
Removing the net slipping is assured a fall.
Knowing when one is laddered up too high,
Stunned back to veracity with a dark sigh.

If ego would stop and freely reach out a hand,
Falls are recoiled by God's band,
Swell the lesser and tend the famine indeed.
With options anew, reconsider and take heed.

The Messenger

He travels the road with beautiful feet,
A smile for all whom he meet.

Out of the world God have called many,
Few who'll work for a penny.

Some begin to preach then become frozen,
Few are they who are chosen.

Many words are spoken but few gets heard,
Some people are rejecting the Word.

Preaching the Gospel for the glory of the Lord,
Wearing a yolk that isn't hard.

There are sacrifices that he must make,
It's not a piece of cake.

Some are preaching for the monetary gift,
Not to give lost souls a lift.

There are some, who live in a lavish house,
Using God's tribute to impress a spouse.

While letting God's house continue to be a shack,
The sheep are falling through the crack.

If it's not of the Lord it will all come to naught,
In his own deceit he'll get caught.

Jesus Is the Only Way

Jesus is the only name by which a man can be saved,
Because of a Father's love the road is paved.

If you call on Him, He'll answer your prayer,
Never leaving or forsaking you He'll always
Be there.

The world is full of confusion and sorrow,
Work for today you're not promised
Tomorrow.

When Jesus comes you don't want to be left,
From your neighbor do not commit theft.

You can't get to heaven being a carnal man,
Hook up with Jesus then you can.

Your body is the Temple of the Holy Ghost,
Of yourself you'll not boast.

True believers of Jesus will walk in the light,
Following Holiness because it's right.

Some people go to Church to jump and shout,
Others wondering what it's about

Jesus is the Truth the Light and the Way,
A ransom for many He did pay.

Preaching for the Money

Be careful what you release from your hand,
False profits are walking the land.
Some messengers will start out on fire,
Being slothful they let it die.

Many have occasionally slipped and fell,
All having a story to tell.
There are those who preach for the money,
Calling another man's wife honey.

Some are always preaching of themselves,
Words of Jesus placed on shelves.
Parading around in a big luxury car,
While members walk from afar.

Living behind the bars of a big fine house,
While being scared as a mouse.
Draining the congregation of every penny,
Meat in Church, there is not any.

Many think they have a piece of cake,
Casting their souls into the lake.
If they don't turn their life around,
Sin will put them in the ground.

Many behind the pulpit have boldly lied,
Love for truth has slowly died.
They're laying up treasures that will rust,
Both will return to dust.

Joining God's Army

They tell me in God's Army, there are Ten Commandments, if you obey them, you shall overcome, yes Lord I want to join.

They tell me in God's Army, many are called, few are chosen, yes Lord I want to join.

They tell me in God's Army, the Lord will fight your battle and victory shall be yours, yes Lord I want to join.

They tell me in God's Army, the women are strong and mighty, a man who fines a wife, finds a good thing, yes Lord, I want to join.

They tell me in God's Army, the food is very good, the bread on the table, is the bread of life, yes Lord I want to join.

They tell me in God's Army, the wine is the best, the drink in the cup, is the blood of Jesus Christ, yes Lord I want to join.

They tell me in God's Army, the water is refreshing, if you drink of this water, you'll never thirst again, yes Lord I want to join.

They tell me in God's Army, the pay is off the chain, endure until the end and you'll be rewarded with a crown of life, yes Lord I want to join.

I'm a soldier of the Lord Jesus Christ

.

My Angel

I tried to go the wrong way, but I was stopped,
My foot the mower almost chopped.
Nervously I sit down on a log to try to think,
Clearing my throat, I took a drink.

As I sat alone thinking about that close call,
My mind raced back to a near fall.
While cleaning off my roof I slipped on a rock,
A gutter nail caught my sock.

When friends and I were camping in the woods,
Thieves broke in and took my goods.
They wounded my neighbor and it is hard to bear,
It could have happened while I was there.

That day I took a short cut across a vacant lot,
I had a feeling that I should not.
Stepping on a rotten board I fell into a large hole,
Almost landed on top of a pole.

The hole was deep very dark and dreary,
My eyes were becoming teary.
I began praying to the Lord for my soul to keep,
Into the hole, water began to seep.

As I lay there on my back confused and crying,
All my hope was slowly dying.
A soft whisper and a strong gentle hand pulled me up,
Saying, because you drank of the Lord's cup.

Stop

Trying to be like the Gofer family and the Hills,
You don't know how they're paying their bills.

Wishing that you could go to the swingers meeting,
You don't know what they're eating.

Wanting to be like Bud cause the girls think he is funny,
You don't know how he makes his money.

Because he walks around flashy you envy old Bob.
That fellow doesn't even have a job.

He just bought a big house, so you want to be like Hank,
You don't know if he hit the lottery or robbed a bank

You wished that you were in Miss Sally's shoes,
Though she's lonely and sick with the blues.

Hoping to be like Sue because she drives a new car,
All night long she hangs at the bar.

Trying to be a con artist like old slick Willie,
Will cause you to look silly.

Stop trying to be like someone else and just be who you are,
Being yourself will take you far.

Rebelling Against God

You disobey the instructions of your father and mother,
While mistreating your sister or brother.
As you are doing it to them you are doing it unto the Lord,
Therefore, making your life hard.

Trying to get to Heaven without Jesus don't even bother,
You reject Him you're rejecting the Father.
Leaders tell us to do something, we mumble and grumble,
Our life takes a downhill tumble.

If God tell us to put something extra in the collection plate,
The preacher we'll begin to hate.
Forgetting that it was the Lord who caused us to be able,
Now we won't help set His table.

God gives to us, but we don't want to give nothing back,
Therefore, we'll begin to lack.
While the Sermon is preached, we'll chew gum and talk,
Some will even get up and walk.

After the messenger has finished preaching to us the Word,
We'll not take heed to what we heard.
We see friends walking, we won't stop and give them a ride,
When they knock, we run and hide.

Never giving a helping hand to those who are sick or in need,
Failing to do a good work or deed.
Always wanting the messenger to let our slothfulness slide,
Of God's law, we'll not abide.

The devil and the lie

Some people are known for talking too much,
Especially when it's about the Church.
They will say things that should not be said,
The devil plays tricks with their head.

Go around spreading gossip and bearing a tale,
Carrying a sign, their soul's for sale.
While saying that it's Jesus whom they follow,
Inside their hearts are hollow.

Saying that you love Jesus but hate your brother,
It's the truth that you smother.
To love one another the Lord told us to do this,
Paul said to greet with a Holy kiss.

Some don't practice what they're preaching,
While others are falsely teaching.
The devil is walking around just laughing at us,
He knows how to keep up a fuss.

We go to Church shout and holler loud on Sunday,
We go to work cursing Monday.
Lying, whore mongering, backbiting, it is all sin,
With Holiness it doesn't fit in.

The devil doesn't mind you faking with your jump and shout,
He knows that in the last day you'll be cast out,
Accept and follow Jesus daily letting old things die,
Make the devil out to be a lie.

Sunday Christian

We are all probably guilty for being one at one time,
Against God, we committed a crime.
Sitting up in Church looking all mighty and proud,
Eyes searching through the crowd.

Looking to see what sister Sally and brother John are doing,
Chastising others while gum you're chewing.
When offering time comes around you never give a dollar,
For a blessing you're the first to holler.

None of your own problems have you ever solved,
In Church business you'll get involved.
To the Lord Jesus Christ you will not let your heart confess,
You go around stirring up mess.

Singing in the choir, but to you no song is ever right,
Always quick to start a verbal fight.
The message from the preacher you call it meddling,
Running from Church to Church, never settling.

Through the week you never give your Bible a second look,
Sunday you might touch the Book.
Party all night Saturday, Sunday the devil puts you to sleep,
You leave the service still a lost sheep.

Through the week for you Bible study and teaching is out,
On Sunday you sit in Church and pout.
Because the preacher won't let you have your way,
In the Church you won't stay.

Caught up in Man's Traditions

The Lord warned us about having such a terrible flaw,
Following the ways of man disregarding God's law.
There is one thing we all must come clean and confess,
Following traditions causes us stress.

The Bible talks about how man observe certain days and things,
Look at the disaster that it usually brings.
If a wife needs to remind her husband of an anniversary date,
She'll often turn it into hate.

We're training our kids to act the same, which is bad,
Not having a birthday party, they become mad.
Men like to do things because it was their father's way,
By-passing the laws of God today.

Some people don't care if they come off like a vulture,
Celebrating someone else's culture.
Some people will celebrate a tradition by getting drunk,
Causing their breath to smell like a skunk.

Children go away to school trying to gain more knowledge,
Traditions have even killed at college.
Man's traditions have caused many of the mighty to fall,
There's not enough paper to write it all.

Follow God's law and get back on the right path,
We all must take a spiritual bath.
Maybe that's why the world is in such bad condition,
Being caught up in man's tradition.

Chosen Vessel Cathedral

I went to Church to hear him preach,
Saw that he could also teach.
In him it wasn't just a lot of idle talk,
He could also do the walk.

The congregation soon let me know,
They were not just for show.
They were all in unity and on one accord,
With joy they all praised the Lord.

Everyone I met treated me like a brother,
They had love one for another.
They were happily walking in the light,
Knowing how to do things right.

Everywhere I went they had turned me down,
The Vessel baptized me without a frown.
The people at Chosen Vessel are very kind,
Chosen vessel was a good find.

I went to Church feeling down, lonely and sad,
When I left, I was bursting from the joy I had.
I was dropped off so that I could get some eats,
At a place called Smokey Pete 's.

As I walked to my Hotel in a slow stride,
A member kindly gave me a ride.
Being a truckdriver I was always on the roam,
Chosen Vessel was my, away Home.

Saint Mable

At the age of 34 she stepped out on faith and never looked back,
Of His helping hand God wasn't slack.
She led her six children down a long and narrow dusty road,
With strength and courage, she carried the load.

She rested her feet in Korhville Texas just south of Tomball,
The people welcomed her, children and all.
After letting her children go off with others to run and play,
A kind woman offered her a place to stay.

Korhville Texas became her place of temporary peace and rest,
Raising her children, she did her best.
God heard her prayers, morning, noon and in the midnight,
She always did that which was right.

It seemed the closer that she would get to the Lord,
The devil tried to make her life hard.
She followed the Lord in being very humble and meek,
She turned to the enemy her left and right cheek.

She raised her children according to the way of God,
On them she didn't spare the rod.
In her house it was so quiet you could hear the clock ticking,
They were in bed early like a chicken.

Sunday mornings off to church she and her children would go,
Her children could never say no.
She taught her children what was right and what was sin,
Grown folk conversations they didn't butt in.

Every neighbor she visited she was met with a warm smile,
They always invited her to stay awhile.
The neighbors treated her children as if being their own,
She knew they'd be cared for when she was gone.

She strived to live her life the way a true Christian should,
In God's sight she did very good.
She stretched out her hand to the passing stranger,
God kept her safe from harm and danger.

Whenever things got hard and she began to lose hope,
God threw her a life-saving rope.
She was a special woman who comes only once in a lifetime,
To the needy she would give her last dime.

Of bad things to say about her there really isn't any,
Of family and friends there are many.
Dry your weeping eyes and wipe away those tears,
God's been grooming her for years.

She finally finished her course and passed the final test,
God has given her that well deserved rest.
Because Mable didn't meddle or cause any strife,
Her name's written in the book of life.

A Man of God (past)

He was a kind and gentle man,
He finished a race well ran.
He lived a life that was plain and simple,
He enjoyed his earthly temple.

He was a man filled with the gift of the Holy Ghost,
Of himself he did not boast.
God didn't just forget and let him be,
He sent an Angel to set him free.

He was a man who never ceased from prayer,
Always beside him his mate was there.
If a thing seemed for him it might be too hard,
He turned it over to Almighty God.

He was not one to just sit around and talk,
He also did the walk.
If by chance he ever called you his friend,
He stood by you until the end.

Because in his heart Jesus did live,
He was willing to forgive.
When the preacher would call on his number,
He didn't sleep or slumber.

In Him God saw a good and righteous seed,
Planting him was a need.
God's the world's Governor He pardons whom He deems fit,
He spared him from the fiery pit.

He was married to a wonderful woman he called honey,
You know he was in love he gave her all his money.
God has taken him to a far better place,
Where men are not separated by race.

In the Kingdom of Heaven there are no flaws,
While on earth he kept God's laws.
Because he treated his fellow man right,
God has made him an everlasting light.

While walking by faith he became a solid rock,
Now he's among the Good Shepherd's flock.
He didn't preach about gossip that he heard,
His message came straight from the Word.

He saw that we are living in the last and evil days,
He preached that man should mend his ways.
This is a truth about him that people can say,
He encouraged those who lost their way.

There is another truth about him that should be spoken,
When he gave his word, it wasn't broken.
Knowing that Jesus was always on his side
When trouble came, he didn't run and hide.

Some people will sit around waiting on a slow train,
While their body ache with pain.
Others are trying to get on board a sinking boat,
The man of God left on a Heavenly float.

The Spirit Knows

While being yet unlearned and clueless of God's Word,
We often will repeat something we heard,
The Spirit knows.

Never giving a second thought to what we have said,
We're often being fooled and mislead,
The Spirit knows.

For no reason one will began to be sad and start to cry,
While silently pondering, to know why,
The Spirit Knows.

We will often use the phrase, "something told me",
Then we'll just let it be,
The Spirit knows.

When one stumbles and starts to go astray,
There's a tug, showing a better way,
The Spirit knows.

When one heats up and gets into a fight,
There's that tug saying it's not right,
The Spirit knows.

God gives us each a Spirit to help us and to guide us,
To keep you out of an unbridled fuss,
The Spirit knows.

When you say "something told me" call Him by name,
In Him there's no shame,
The Spirit knows.

The Spirit knows when we're taking the wrong road,
The Spirit knows when we're about to overload.
The Spirit knows.

 The Spirit cries for us because He knows what's coming;
The Spirit knows why grandma was humming,
The Spirit knows.

 The Spirit knows that we must walk in the light,
The Holy Spirit will only do, that which is right,
The Spirit knows.

Chapter 2

Love

A Mother (A Gift from God)

God created man and thought it was not good for him to be alone,
So, He created him a mate from his bone.
A woman was formed a beautiful sight for all the world to see,
God formed her to a perfect Tee.

God said to the woman and man, go, be fruitful and multiply,
Today the woman catches every man's eye.
Because of God's blessing and her fruitfulness, the woman became
a Mother,
She nourishes her children and teaches them to love one another.

Even after the children have grown and left the comforts of the nest,
A Mother never gets that well deserved rest.
Not only do she reach out to the children, but she cares for the big
Baby she calls Honey,
When the man gets a little ache, he acts like he's dying, sometimes
it's funny.

A Mother's work in her household, from work to caring and loving,
is never ending,
The children and her spouse's bumps and bruises, she's always mending.
A Mother's love is sweeter than any apple pie or cotton candy,
For her children, she's never out of reach, she always handy.

Besides God, a Mother is the greatest gift that a man and child can
have and share,
When you need support, be it moral or physical, she's always there.
A Mother's hugs are fitting and tighter than the finest glove,
A Mothers hugs are warm, comforting and full of love.

Brothers, sisters and children, love and respect your Mother in all
your ways,
Strive to make her life pleasing and happy all her days.
A Mother will stick by you when no one else will,
For a child's mishaps she'll foot the bill.

Remember men, honor and cherish your beautiful Mother,
She goes beyond that extra mile, like no other.
A Mother's love is spread, given and tested throughout her life
She's not just a Mother, she's also a loving wife.

A Father

God created man in His own image, gave him life, a job,
specific instructions and then a mate,
Now this is where man meets his fate.

The man was happy, he had a mate, an easy job, running around in
the Garden of Eden foot loose and fancy free,
One day he disobeyed God's instructions and let his mate
talk him into eating from the forbidden tree.

Because he was hardheaded, he lost his easy job, was kicked
from the premises and had to learn to till the ground,
Now he had to eat by the sweat of his brow, the pitta patter of
little feet would soon be around.

With the arrival of a child man became a Father, continuing
to be fruitful and working the land,
With a wife and children, a Father can't just sit around with
his feet in the sand.

A good, God fearing Father will have the patience of Job who
lost all that he had,
Like Abraham, his faith won't waver when the times get bad.
A good Father will have the love of the prodigal son's Father,
When a wayward child returns home, it won't be a bother.

A Godly Father will have the love of Joseph and the heart of
Nehemiah who worked for the King,
When life knocks him down, he will get up and step back in the ring.
Being a good Father is not always a bed of roses and cruises,
He will encounter Fatherhood's, bumps and bruises.

First comes the mate who is known as the wife, with all the little,
Honey dos,
That's when husbands make those muffled, and silent 'boos

Coming home from work a Father must be prepared for those
unforeseen household chores,
Not after he rest, but the minute he walks through those doors

Sometimes when Fathers get together, they do a little bragging,
But in raising children some Fathers are behind and lagging.
A good Father loves God, his wife and his children, in that order,
From these ways, he doesn't cross that border.

He loves his wife and brings up his children in the way that they should go,
The fear of God he will teach them to know.
On his child, a good Father will not spare the rod,
To discipline a child is the way of God.

Wives, love your husband he is the Father of your children and head
of the house,
Stand beside him, help him to not stray and become a louse.
Children, love your Father and make him proud,
Don't get caught up with the wrong crowd.

Now some Fathers have become Elders, Pastors and gospel preachers,
Others have become deacons and Sunday school teachers.
Some are elevated to Bishops and Prophets, all ending with a great story,
All Fathers, regardless of occupation or position should give God the Glory.

"Fathers love the Lord, your wives and children, remember, work while
it is day and be of good cheer."

Love

God in Heaven is the author of true love,
Sending it down from above.

Planting the seed in the Garden of Eden,
Woman wasn't made to be beaten.

Given for all people of the world to share,
In each heart it should be there.

Love will not turn its back on a friend,
A broken heart it'll mend.

The way you love will determine your fate,
Love isn't a product of hate.

Does not tear families and friends apart,
It'll melt the iciest heart.

Love will take time to go and visit the sick,
Love doesn't have no certain pick.

Love is always kind to every passing stranger,
Never putting innocence in danger.

Love will always respect and honor a mother,
It'll never hurt or kill a brother.

Having love for us have hid a multitude of sin,
God's love will always win.

Bearing Love's Hurt

Absorbing harsh insults, receiving an unexpected punch,
Not understanding onlookers pondering, asking why? A
friend with whom one is so often sharing lunch.

Children rebelling, in-laws hating, spouses are cheating,
No measure of apologies, not even an unbridled check,
Could one put on the times a lonely heart takes a beating.

Eyes that cries in vain, no one sees the damage that is so deep,
From mere words that have been tossed and hurled so often,
Causing one to lose many nights sleep.

During an offense, sticking beside them is a mother's way,
Though she'll cry a lot, even lose all her life's savings,
She'll be waiting patiently on the appointed day.

Quietly she suffers the constant abuse of an unjust man,
Her soul being tormented day and night, pondering her plight,
She raises her children the best she can.

Unwilling to give a love one time to reform in jail,
Praying that the Lord will change his demeanor,
Continues to live in a place of irrepressible hell.

Feels at times like being pressed down and tied with a rope,
Stepped on, looked over, never even given a kind word,
Because of love, she never gives up hope.

Because one is hardened, to you seems a slight confused,
You can't see just by looking at the outward view, If a
friend is suffering or being inaudibly abused.

Enjoying Spring Season

While slowly awakening to the quietness of my room,
my eyes eagerly pushing open their lids, anxious to
see what the new day would bring. My ears faintly
picks up the harmony of birds singing from a distant,
while my hands gently wipe away the sleep from my eyes,
as they capture pieces of a broken broom.

With a little resistance my legs are hesitating to leave
the bed while my feet are racing to reach the floor.
After it's all said and done my body is ready to go out
and enjoy the sunshine just on the other side of the
shaded glass door.

As I open the door and step out onto the patio, I slowly
breathe in a deep breath of fresh air that's filled with
the aroma of springs early blossoms while love songs are
playing on the radio.

My lungs welcome the arrival of freshly scented spring
air, ahh, the beauty of spring season; oh, how I wish it never
had to end, that every day spring could begin all anew.
In the spring the sun gives us light and helps the flowers
and gardens to grow, soaking up the morning dew.

Flowers being so beautiful and scented, with a fresh aroma
that spread throughout all the land, for all to look upon
and enjoy. The air in the spring is like precious stones that
everybody loves to enjoy, maybe even own it and hold it
in their hand.

The farmers are planting, and the vegetables are growing, this
is the time of the season that the magic of love is filling the air,
and the weddings bells began making a showing.

Love birds are getting engaged, romances are blooming, weddings
are happening all over. I'm in love with the joys of spring and
all the good things that it brings for the young and the aged, so,
enjoy what spring brings your way, don't throw away that
four leaf clover.

Something About Butterfly
(A beautiful black woman)

She's the diamond that stands alone,
Giving light where none is shown.
Moves like a leaf floating to the ground,
Touching earth without making a sound.

Hair like sassy black silk on a drying line,
For her men's heart race and pine.
Graced with a beautiful smile that shines so bright;
Shames the Moon and puts the sun to flight.

She makes a blind man wish that he could see,
The beautiful lily God formed her to be.
Makes an old man savor his golden days,
A young man ventures forbidden ways.

Skin like chocolate dipped in a special caramel,
Never to be found in a fairytale.
With eyes like rubies and teeth like pearls,
She's not proud like most beautiful girls.

With lips like Heavenly grown peach slices,
Having an aroma better than spices.
A body soft as a pillow where one may sleep,
Placing in her bosom his heart to keep.

Having even a deeper beauty than the eye can see,
There's none lovelier a woman for me.
My home is blessed with a perfect "10"
I have a Butterfly Gracing my Den.

Things A Wife Does

The first person to wake and get out of bed,
Removing the nightcap from her head.
Quietly she rushes to take a quick shower,
Walks to the kitchen on reserve power.

She struggles hard to fix a perfect meal,
Cooking the meat on a grille.
Makes sure the kids are ready for school,
Volunteers for the carpool.

Not many peaceful moments in her life,
It's a fulltime job being a wife.
Respecting her husband, she tries to please,
Sometimes he's just a tease.

Off to the store to do the grocery shopping,
Back at home it's time for mopping.
When evening comes and the kids are back,
She's ready to hit the sack.

Before her husband gets home from work,
She lets the coffee perk.
Constantly she's screaming at the kids,
Stirring pots and lifting lids.

At the end of the day she has grown tired,
Feels like her body's been fried.
Quietly she's taking it in her own way,
Tomorrow will be another day.

The Pensive Letter

Why's she writing an early Dear John?
Reading one of these is never fun.

When I finish reading, I'll know why,
She decided to dump this guy.

Judging the way these words are written,
She is not a happy kitten.

Never mentions the good times they had,
She only reminds him of the bad.

Reminded of words that he had spoken,
I know his heart will be broken.

Because of him being handsome and nice,
She wanted to pass under the rice.

Feeling rejected she wants him to hurt,
She's dating his friend Bert.

I'll do the best I can to delay the pain,
Maybe I'll wash off in the rain.

When the mail carrier stops off to eat,
Maybe I'll slip under the seat.

This part of the job causes me to quiver,
This one message I hate to deliver.

Spring in a Bottle

Getting out of bed I reached for my bottle of joy,
Like a kid on Christmas with a new toy.

Slowly I begin twisting on the tightly sealed cap,
Loosening after I give it a tap.

Placing it in the center of the window on a ledge,
Careful not to drop it off the edge.

The first to burst forth are the rays of sun light,
Removing darkness from the night.

Then comes the aroma of the flowers,
Followed closely by April showers.

Fresh air comes floating out on a cloud,
Hanging low and smelling proud.

Last out, comes the harmony of the birds,
Can't be described by mere words.

Springtime gives everything a reason for glowing,
Gardens make a real good showing.

The spirit of love flourishes in full bloom,
A time when a girl finds a groom.

We all love the beautiful days of spring,
A season only God can bring.

Because God Loves Me

He wakes me up on time each dawn,
Giving me the ability to yawn.

Though I may be blind he opens my eyes so that I can see,
The plan He's laid out for me.

Even if I don't have the use of both my feet,
He opens my mouth so I can eat.

Without a natural voice I can still talk,
Having no legs, I'm able to walk.

Without physically speaking I can cry out and pray,
Thanking God for another day.

With deaf ears I'm still able to hear,
With ducts I can shed a tear.

From His messenger I've already heard,
Arm myself with the Word.

With my own tongue I'm able to confess,
Ask Jesus my soul to bless.

Able to distinguish between good and bad,
Thanking God for the life I've had.

God, my Heavenly Father didn't just make me and let me be,
His love is more than just what eyes can see.

Let God Choose Your Mate

We rush into a relationship being blind,
God is the least on our mind.

Choosing a mate because of their look,
Hoping that they can cook.

The saying, what you see is what you get,
Most people haven't learned yet.

If a man can sing harmony with the birds,
He flatters women with his words.

An athlete who is at the top of his game,
A girl will marry him for money and fame.

Gold diggers will sink their hooks in deep,
Marriage vows they'll not keep.

You picked a mate who is not home at night,
Everyday you're in a fight.

It is very hard trying to keep a good house,
When you're married to a louse.

Everything that is good comes from above,
Wait for God to send your love.

When you have a Saint for a spouse,
There'll be peace in your house.

You and your mate would still be clicking,
Had you let God do the picking.

If you let God's hand deliver your fate,
You'll get the perfect mate.

If the World Was One Color

Could we survive if we were all the same?
Having only one racial name.

What if all our bodies were of one shade,
Do you think we'd have it made?

There would be ado about the color to be,
Keep reading and you'll see.

Some of the people will let out a loud bark,
Not that color it's too dark.

There are others who'll cry that it's too light,
Only God knows what's right.

We would all be wearing the same boots,
Having no need to trace our roots.

Now on the other side of that same plate,
This is where we meet our fate.

There would be no difference in the food,
We'd all be in the same mood

Being a different color is a very good thing,
Watch the flowers in the spring.

Look at the leaves on the trees in the fall,
God love colors of all.

Sometimes after the rain, appears a rainbow,
Regardless of color, let love flow.

God made us from one of His master plans,
He saw it good to have multiple clans.

Family Reunion

God made man and saw that he was alone,
He created him a mate from his bone.

He commanded them to be fruitful and multiply
The seed of life comes with a cry.

Man, woman and child became a family bonded,
Tied by love that God funded.

For one another a family should always pray,
Even when one lives far away.

Man will leave his parents and cleave to his wife,
Together they'll start a new life.

God said, a man who finds a wife finds a good thing,
The heart rejoices for the joy she'll bring.

The torch is passed to carry on the family name,
Every kin must bear the blame.

A family should always have love one for another,
Never turning away a brother.

A family's bond should be stronger than leather,
The power of love binding them together.

Family should call, send a card or make a drive down,
Doing it with a smile not with a frown.

Kin should come together keeping the bond alive,
The Family Reunion rates a high five.

A Trucker's Life

Sitting behind the wheel most of their days,
Truckers travel different ways.
A target for every money grabbing being,
An easy life they're not seeing.

Driving days and sometimes into the night,
Entering places that are tight.
Taking verbal hits and being constantly abused,
By some companies they're misused.

Being awaken by a harlot knocking on the door,
Not caring that its around four.
Hoping to chase her off with a very loud tone,
In a quick flash she's gone.

Always on the go and being away from home,
Sleeping inside a mobile dome.
No one seems to care or understand truckers,
Being tagged as dumb suckers.

Most things in the Truck Stop has a high price tag,
Causing a lot of truckers to gag.
Shopping at a super center is becoming the thing,
Low prices make their hearts sing.

Life as a truck driver is not a bed of roses,
At them people turn up their noses.
The police lay in wait to catch them off guard,
Issuing tickets hitting them hard.

They run hard to make every delivery on time,
Always struggling for every dime.
There are obstacles trying to empty their pocket,
If they speed the police clock-it.

A trucker's life is filled with lots of paperwork,
Don't get a dispatcher who acts like a jerk.
While some are known to tell a few lies,
With the truth they have no ties.

In a trucker's life there's a lot of hurry up and wait,
Long lines they began to hate.
Tempers began to flare and there are verbal fights,
They forget about all rights.

Truckers take freight from point A to point B,
Delivering things for you and me.
Everything in your home by a truck it was sent,
Of hating truckers, you must repent.

Truckers are human and will make some mistakes,
It's no reason to jam your brakes.
Truck drivers take a lot of crap and constant heat,
Dangers on the road they often meet.

Every day they crank up, their lives are on the line,
Swerving to miss a fool, full of wine.
Driving a truck is full of decisions that are quick,
The fog and traffic both get thick.

In rain or sleet a trucker is still dispatched to go,
Even when there's a heavy snow.
A truck driver's job should be viewed with pride,
Truck driving can be a lonely ride.

A Husband's dilemma

A husband works hard to make a living for the wife,
His is not always a happy life.

On her birthday he buys her a ring,
She calls it a raggedy thing.

His purpose is to make her happy,
But she's always snappy.

Every day she complains and nag,
With his love she plays tag.

Everything her girlfriends do or say is right,
Like a setting hen, she's ready to fight.

He even bought her, her first new car,
All she does is hang out at the bar.

When he come home there's no food on the table,
She sits around all day watching cable.

When he asks why the house isn't clean,
She becomes very mean.

His love for her has been tried,
It's time she was fired.

Her whirlwind romance has come to an end,
Tell that to your girlfriend.

A Foolish Child

Disobeys the instructions of a father and mother,
Doesn't get along with a sister or brother.
Not willing to adhere to discipline and strict rules,
Get expelled from all schools.

Run away from home without giving any thought,
Tangled in street life he's caught.
Without a secure or warm place to lay his head,
He begins to miss his bed.

Missing and longing for the family he loves so dear,
Lonely and afraid he sheds a tear.
Seeing and hearing a lot of scary things in the night,
He now knows running away wasn't right.

Getting pressure from a girl friend or some boy,
A girl will give up her secret joy.
A slick talking boy lays her down in the dirt,
Telling lies to get under her skirt.

Skipping her childhood in a heated rush to be grown,
Now she's scared and on her own.
Hating herself for listening to all those well delivered lies,
She can't rest because the baby cries.

She didn't listen to the advice her mother was giving,
Now she's having a hard time living.
Because you failed to listen to your parent's advice,
Now you must pay the price.

A Foolish Woman

She gets pregnant to try to keep a man,
Hoping he doesn't turn on the fan. (run)
Falls in love with a man without a job,
Sticks to him like corn on a cob.

She'll stay around and take the beatings,
While he goes to AA meetings.
Every time he comes back, there's no change,
She refuses to leave his range.

A good man she'll openly mistreat and use,
His love and kindness she'll abuse.
Constantly screaming and barking a command,
Pushing him into sinking sand.

She's married but she hangs out like a single girl,
In clubs and bars giving it a whirl.
Never giving her husband a moment of piece,
Keeping him on a short lease.

Shamelessly giving her body to his supposed to be friend,
Crying because the marriage will end.
For a night with the girls and a rump in the hay,
She drove a loving husband away.

Because she chose to travel down the wide road,
She's left to carry the load.
Disobeying God's Law and playing the field,
She suffers before her heart is healed.

Life or Drugs

Early each morning I get on my knees and pray,
Asking the Lord to keep me from temptations,
that I may cause no hurt or sorrow as I go
Through the day.

When I go to work at the beginning of the day,
I give the man what I promised for the money
he's willing to pay.

I live a very peaceful and drug free life,
I am happy living in the city with the
children and wife.

You must be careful of the road you choose,
If you go down the drug trail, you are sure to
lose.

Drugs are destroying lives and killing people each
day, why do so many go down that dangerous
way?

Drugs rob the poor and gives to the fast and greedy,
Oftentimes, taking away from a family that is
needy.

To your body, be very careful what you give,
If it's a long and happy life that you're
desiring to live.

Life is a precious gift to us from the Lord,
It's your choice whether you make it easy
or hard.

A Foolish Man

He'll do things so that he can be seen,
To some people he's very mean.
Arguing and fighting with a sister or brother,
He'll turn against his mother.

Unwilling to learn anything while in school,
He thinks quitting is something cool.
Hooked on drugs from his family he steals,
Day after day making drug deals.

Having a long and hard time finding a job,
He walks around being a slob.
Has a wife, who is very loving and sweet,
On the table he puts no meat.

Knowing that he has the love of his life,
Often abusing a very sweet wife.
Because he lost the good woman that he had,
He mopes around being sad.

By making the choice of being a lazy louse,
He loses a wonderful spouse.
Because he chose to break the Lord's Rule,
He ends up a lonely fool.

A Special Book (Bible)

You browsed around for hours looking for me,
I'm everything you need me to be.

You always stayed a step or two ahead of the pack,
Hoping you wouldn't have to come back.

Thumbing through the pages at record speed,
I'm something that you need.

While waiting patiently in the long check-out line,
A few of the patrons began to whine.

When you got home you got a call from Nancy,
Something else caught your fancy.

After a while when you were quiet and not talking,
You picked me up and started walking.

Then after a while you finished with your call,
You laid me atop a shelf on the wall.

I watch every day as you continually pass me bye,
If I had tear ducts I would cry.

As time passes on, I'm missing your gentle touch,
I'm a book, use me as such.

In the store I thought you were a quick learner,
Now you've put me on the back burner.

Opening me up you can gain a world of knowledge,
I should be placed in every college.

What's written in me is what you need,
For your heart I'll always plead.

Rainy Days

When it rained mother would make us
come inside the house,
And when it was thundering, she made
us be quiet as a mouse.

We had to lay down with a blanket on
the floor and take a nap,
If you failed to adhere to the rule your
backside got a tap.

As I grew older, I learned about all the
good things that rain do,
Like the life water it supplies for people
and things too.

The birds use rainwater to take a bath,
home to the fish and a traveling path.
Leaves a rainbow in the sky,
which can be seen by the naked eye.

Rain gives life to the May flowers,
They're watered by the April
showers.

Rain is also a well-known narrator of sleep.
Water in our body we must keep,
There's water in winter and in the spring,
It's God doing a great thing.

When I Was Young

Like most boys my age I enjoyed going to school,
We had a principal who was cool.
The school building was made of cedar wood,
In math and spelling I did good.

I always walked to school with the rest of the bunch,
Some days I had no lunch.
During my chores at home was not too hard,
Working didn't interfere with my report card.

Growing up under a mother who served the Lord,
Doors and windows were never barred.
Every Sunday morning to Church we all would go,
We didn't have a choice of saying no.

Grown up conversations, children didn't butt in,
Disrespecting your elders was a sin.
When we were in Church, we didn't run and play,
Sunday was considered the Lord's day.

The people were always singing and jumping with joy,
To Church we didn't take a toy.
While the preacher was preaching, we sit very quiet,
As if being on a no talking diet.

My mother raised her children according to God,
She didn't ever spare the rod.
At a time, blacks and whites didn't use the same table,
Today we sit side by side watching cable.

A Good Neighbor

He'll answer the door whenever you knock,
Your boat he'll never rock.

He'll always be there to lend a helping hand,
He'll help to work your land.

Being good and faithful because he love it,
Another's wife he won't covet.

If you go to his home very late in the night,
He'll always do what's right.

Family members puff up and start to moan,
He'll gladly give you a loan.

He'll treat your children as if they were his own,
Never using a harsh tone.

He won't envy you because of your new car,
Being envious will cause a scar.

He greets all his neighbors with a big smile,
Invites them over to sit awhile.

Never will he be coldhearted and cast them out,
Loving your neighbor is what it's about.

Chapter 3

Humor

Once upon a time in Korhville Texas

There was a very mischievous boy back in the day,
He was a bad little fellow down Korhville way.

For those who did not know him, he was a character and a half,
He knew what to do to make you laugh.

He grew up on Carter road walking barefoot in the sand,
At a window he would throw a rock and hide his hand.

When the person came running out, before they asked who,
He was already pointing at you.

He would get you in trouble and then laugh like a cackling chicken,
While your mother was giving you a good licking.

If there was a bad kid dictionary with the word Boogie Bear,
A picture of him would be there.

He used to always tease a bowlegged woman named Mrs. Pip,
One day a wasp came along and stung him on the lip.

There was the time that he was trying to pass a note,
The principle took it to see what he had wrote.

It was a poem to a girl who lived in Tomball,
The principle read it before us all.

It read, I love you Bip, I love you Bop, .
I love you more than a hog love Slop.

The Freight Shaker

If you want to have yourself some fun,
Get yourself a Freight shaker son.

Not to call any names, I'll let you put one to it,
So, this is how we going to do it.

If the other trucks can't make it up the hill,
You can bet a Freight shaker will.

There is one thing that you should all know,
Some trucks were built for show.

Freight shakers pulls their loads very good,
While others are wishing they could.

While some trucks might be a little fast,
Against a Freight shaker, they can't last.

When you pass by them trucks, tip your hat,
They're not use to that.

We must put all the tales and rumors to rest,
Freight shaker trucks are the best.

A good truck pulling on its best day,
With a Freight shaker it can't stay.

Up the tallest mountain a Freight shaker will go,
While the others wait for a tow.

Freight shaker drivers are smooth operators,
All other drivers are imitators.

Now if the other driver had brains and was smart,
He would've driven a Freight shaker from start.

When the others are rusted and put under ground,
The Freight shaker will still be around.

If you're wise, let Freight shaker take you to school,
So that you don't end up being a fool.

 Last, but not least in the trucking world you'll find,
A Freight shaker gives you peace of mind.

The CB Rambo

The CB Rambo is in no shape to brag,
We all know he's just a scrag.

At being a professional he's a bit slow,
That's a word he doesn't know.

Talking trash on the CB and hiding in the sack,
He can't rest for watching his back.

One day he'll make a mistake and slip,
Then he'll get a busted lip.

We know that he's not a real true trucker,
He's just one dumb sucker.

The CB Rambo can't talk upon a wife,
Therefore, having no sex life.

He's always doing things that are very dumb,
Proving that his mind is numb.

The CB Rambo is one who's full of flaws,
Talking trash and breaking laws.

He'll always be known as just a CB Rambo,
Having nowhere to go.

The CB Rambo is a very sad and lonely man,
Causing strife wherever he can.

The CB Rambo's destiny is to always roam,
Having no place to call home.

The day is coming when he'll get his in the end,
For now, he's just blowing wind.

A Big Truck's Tale

Well, here we go down the road without a plan,
I hope we're not caught by the man.
The last time this guy tried to take a short cut,
He ended up looking like a nut.

He tried going down a steep hill out of gear,
We hit a little truck in the rear.
I tried braking for him, but I had a heavy load,
We weren't on a big truck road.

I can tell when my driver has been drinking,
He makes moves without thinking.
I really hate it when he drives too fast,
At that speed we won't last.

He wrecked me so many times that it's not funny,
The courts get all his money.
To top it off he sleeps with an unknown stranger,
Putting his own life in danger.

Cranking up and not checking to see what I need,
It'll cause him headaches indeed.
I'm a big truck and should be treated as such,
Is that asking too much?

Texts Bar-B-Que

There's nothing like a good Bar-B-Que,
Enjoyed by many cooked by few.

Word of good Que covers a lot of ground,
People come from miles around.

While the women are in the house chilling,
The men are outside grilling.

If you go to a Que and can't smell it in the air,
If I were you, I wouldn't eat there.

Not anybody just can put on an apron and burn,
There's lots you need to learn.

Cooking good Que is not a hurry up rush job,
You can't boil it like corn on the cob.

Well-cooked meat won't fight you for the bone,
Anything less, leave it alone.

There are many imitators roaming the land,
Cooking Que gritty like sand

When dating a girl and you're not good looking,
Win her over with good Que-cooking.

If you think you can hang with the best,
Put your burning skills to the test.

If your Que has a real good flavor and taste,
None of it will go to waste.

When your Que apron has turned into a rag,
Then you've earned the right to brag.

If you want good Que, Houston TX is the place to be,
If you don't believe it come and see.

Try Being A Dog

Come on boy go fetch the ball,
That's so off the wall.

Instead of you shaking your head,
Why don't you play dead?

You'll ask me to sit up and beg,
Although I'm missing a leg.

Instead of giving me some meat,
You throw me a bone I can't eat.

Let me put a chain on your neck,
See if you'll give a heck.

In the summer when it's real hot,
Be confined to one spot.

Being tied up and forgotten a few days,
I bet that'll change your ways.

Going a couple days without any water,
Makes playing a lot harder.

With all the needy things that I lack,
You want me to walk the track.

You let my body be home to the flea,
Doing nothing, you let it be.

On a dog, human beings will run a con,
A dog's work is never done.

If you think a dog's life is a lot of fun,
You've had too much sun.

A Shoe's Tale

A lot of people take care of their feet,
There are some who aren't so neat.
Some will try to squeeze an eleven into a ten,
Knowing that it won't fit in.

Like a kid trying to put a square into an O,
They should see that it won't go.
My shape is tired of being stretched out,
I'm cut up because of gout.

Trying to wear a shoe that can't be worn,
Causes your foot to have a corn.
My skin's been stretched in so many ways,
I'm just counting my days.

Some people have feet that smell so bad,
Causes my tongue to be sad.
People that I saw were heavy and light,
Bought shoes that were too tight.

The person that wears me his name is Ned,
He keeps me underneath the bed.
Man! How his feet really do stink,
I need a real stiff drink.

I've been kicked and dragged over the ground,
By this time tomorrow I won't be around.
It'll do Ned no good to look for me later,
I'm doing like the alligator.

The left shoe won't come but that's all right,
It won't cause us to fight.
Tonight, I'm catching the first train smoking,
This is one shoe that's not joking.

Stolen Money

I hope this fellow is trying to cast a vote,
Uh oh, it's a hold-up note.
From underneath his coat he pulled a gun,
Screaming people began to run.

He's nervously barking out loud commands,
Making waving gestures with his hands.
The helicopters were beginning to hover,
The cashiers ran for cover.

Giving one cashier an empty bag to fill,
Stating he wouldn't hesitate to kill.
After stuffing all big bills into the bag,
He covered it up with a rag.

There was an accomplice he called Gus,
Quickly trying to count us,
A bank teller thought that he was quick,
The robbers were just too slick.

We sped down the road passing a waiting cop,
I think I heard a tire pop.
We've been stolen by some of the best,
None has ever passed the test.

You have given the DA a solid case,
It's too late to hide your face,
Although you didn't shoot your gun,
Your case can't be won.

When you go to the courtroom tomorrow,
It'll be the beginning of sorrow.
Remember when they ship you off to the pen,
Stay out of big Bubba's den.

I hope you learned that crime doesn't pay,
Look where you're at today.
Remember when it's time for you to get out,
Robbing isn't what life's about.

The Little Ant

I may be little and tiny, but I can make an elephant sneeze,
Bring the strongest man to his knees.

Instead of finger popping I work hard those long summer days,
When winter arrives, that hard work pays.

The grasshopper struts around doing nothing during summer,
Every winter for him it's a bummer.

People are not any smarter when they stand on top of my mound,
I give them a bite, making them holler and I don't weigh a pound.

I may be small and tiny, but I pack a mean punch,
Not being careful I might have you for lunch

I love it when people drop sweet stuff and I get a sugar rush,
Hey, they didn't need to know that, boy hush.

Well, they say one man's junk is another man's treasure,
Maybe I shouldn't bite them their food gives me pleasure.

I may not be built tough, but I can carry a load,
I can even cross over a flooded road.

They say that men are strong and mighty, but I don't know why,
When little old me can make the toughest one cry.

Now I don't mind them stepping over or going around my bed,
That way I won't have to play rat a tat-tat on that head.

Listen up my friend and take heed, this is not just a rant,
You should know by now beware of the ant.

Zoo Animals

You brought them little bad kids to the zoo,
I'm a monkey and I throw poo.

Now you had all better beware of my strong cousin the Gorilla,
Sometimes he gets out, turning your visit into a thriller.

Be very careful around the cage of that old slippery snake,
If he grabs you, from his grip you cannot shake.

Beware of that old slick Llama he will try to spit in your eye,
The Baboon will hit you with a freshly dropped pie.

When you visit and we are not out yet, here's what that mean,
We are not ready to be seen.

Whatever you do don't fall into that sneaky alligator lake,
They will quickly carve you up like a steak.

While some of the birds here at the zoo makes a lot of noise,
The Peacocks struts their stuff in a graceful poise.

The Giraffe is a very tall animal that people love to see,
To me he's not all that, he squats to pee.

Because I'm a Monkey and not the brightest bulb in the lamp,
But in this Zoo, I am the Champ.

The Wise Cat

I don't mind being a house cat or someone's precious pet,
But why a dog? I haven't figured that out yet.

The silly dog runs around the house chasing its tail,
Showing us all that its mind is not well.

The dog does not know how to follow a simple rule,
All through the house he will bark and drool.

Now us cats we're very quiet, tidy and clean,
We like our food to be tasty and lean.

A cat loves to eat some good tuna fish,
We also like warm milk in a dish.

Every now and then I will venture out to catch a bird,
I'm telling you what I know, you have my word.

A stray dog jumped me as I walked across the yard,
Against that beast I had to fight hard.

I had to do something because day was turning to night,
It seemed that I was losing the fight.

With all my might I hit him with a right claw,
During that instance I saw his flaw.

I grazed his nose with the left claw, that dog left there running,
Against that mutt I was just too cunning.

If you don't want to be stuck with a pet that's sloppy and fat,
Get yourself a clean and tidy cat.

A Cat's Worse Nightmare

Yeah, I am a dog and here is what I have to say,
I can beat a cat on any given day.

I sat and I listened to what that cat said he did,
Every cat I ever fought ran and hid.

The best advice that I could give you is to run,
Because if I catch you it won't be fun.

Just let one of them tomcats try to cross my lawn,
I'll be all over them from dusk to dawn.

When he tries to run, I'll grab his tail with my powerful jaw,
Swing him around and hit him with my paw.

Then before I let go, I'll let out a loud victory bark,
Slamming him to the ground causing a spark.

Now you know by this dog, down the road that old cat was sent,
Running so fast, you couldn't see which way he went

For weeks he'll lick his wounds while hiding from his pals,
Being too ashamed to show his face around the gals.

In case you all don't know, most Tomcats fight like a little girl,
That old Tomcat's mama should have named him Pearl.

Whenever he ventures out again, he'll tell every cat in sight,
That Rottweiler is one dog you don't want to fight.

A Crooked Neck

If only you didn't have such a hard head,
You wouldn't be looking half dead.

I tried telling you that position wasn't right,
You tossed and turned all night.

You can't move your head that way,
I'm inflicting pain today.

If you would've listened to what I said,
You'd be at work and not in bed.

Because you refused to change your pillow,
Now you're like a weeping willow.

One way to get rid of me and back to work,
Give your head a quick Jerk.

You must treat me as if I'm nitro glistering,
Maybe next time you'll be listening.

From now on be very careful how you sleep,
The next crook you'll have to keep.

The Rebellious Mouth

Because you were young and didn't know any better,
I didn't force you to adhere to the letter.

Now that you've graduated you think you're grown,
The rules change when you step out on your own.

I know lately that things have been a little tense,
But you're supposed to have some sense.

You put things in me that you know you should not,
Even after I tell you they're too hot.

You pretend you don't know what I'm talking about,
If it's bad, I'll spit it out.

Trying to force me to eat meat that's burned black,
I'm going to throw it back.

I've seen how some of the food has been treated,
There's no way I'm going to eat it.

Every now and then you want to take a little dip,
I'm not keeping that under my lip.

I don't even know why you're trying to smoke,
Knowing it causes me to choke.

If you don't start eating a healthy meal,
This mouth I'm going to seal.

The Quiet One

He grew up in Cypress Texas which we called the Woods,
With their neighbors they shared their goods.

He was surrounded by a host of sisters and brothers,
Raised by one of the Churches strictest of mothers.

Now some of the clan were a wild and rowdy bunch,
They traveled in numbers and packed a mean punch.

Wherever they went it was like the days of Doc Holiday and Wyatt,
But he was more shy, calmer and quiet.

One thing for sure is that his life was very enchanting,
Every night in her yard his feet he was planting.

You could see him coming down that old dusty, bumpy dirt road,
On his old Ford, he wore out 2 sets of shocks carrying the load.

You could tell he was crazy in love because the Woods wasn't that far,
When he came to visit her instead of going home, he slept in his car.

There were three people in Korhville Texas who drove real, real, real, slow
He was one of the three we all came to know.

A trip for him to the Barbershop in Acres Holmes took him almost a
half day,
You could give him 2 hours head start and still pass him along
the way.

Trailing Memories

Living out in the country after school we would go berry picking,
Talking back to your elders got your backside a licking.

We would follow the gully to our little muddy swimming hole,
Some carried a homemade fishing pole.

The sun beaming down on the road made it very hot,
It was steaming like water boiling in a pot.

If you couldn't swim, you'd better not get close to the water then,
The older guys would throw you in.

On our way home we'd grab a couple of an old farmer's melons,
It's a wonder we didn't turn out to be felons.

We were just ordinary kids being mischievous country boys,
Growing up in the 50's and 60's making our own toys.

Growing up in the country we had a lot of fun,
When it got too hot, we stayed out of the sun.

Out in the country there was no pool or recreational park,
Wherever we played we had to be back before dark.

Some fruits grew wild in the woods and we'd eat too many,
Down at the little corner store cookies were 2 for a penny.

Parents were very strict on girls, if you got a kiss you did good,
You'd count your good fortune and knock on wood.

Living in the country with your neighbors you lived as one,
Committing crimes against a neighbor there was none.

Back in the day in the country we slept in peace,
Now we wonder will the violence ever cease.

A Great Basketball Player

A man who knows the game of basketball and plays it well,
He gives the world a great story to tell.
He is having the greatest time and a wonderful life,
Enjoying the fruits of his labor with his kids and wife.

He is a great person, athlete and humanitarian, he's one in a million,
A man who could make as much as a trillion.
He is a son, husband, father, athlete and a man with a heart of Gold,
All over the World his feats and story shall be told.

Like a light in the darkest of nights giving its beam,
He shines on any given team.
He makes the impossible of basketball shots seem like a breeze,
He does it with such grace and ease.

While barreling down the court his opponents hears a sound like a train humming,
They turn to look and it's just him coming
No man on this earth is perfect, but he does strive,
While coming down the lane for a drive.

In the World of athletes and non-athletes alike, it is a fact,
On our lives he makes a big impact.
Some of his shots causes his opponents to want to cry,
Leaving them in awe as he lets one fly.

When on the basketball court and the ball is in his hands he's greatly feared,
Cutting them down to size while they stand looking weird.
Going in for a layup he passes by his opponents in a dash.
Leaving behind the twin shadows of a splash.

He flies high above the rim it hardly seems fair
Removing the remnants left by the air.
When in doubt and up against the wall,
Give the greatest player the ball.

On any given night from his hands the points are going to rain,
Causing his opponents agony and pain.
There is one thing for sure his Legacy is here to stay,
Basketball is one game that he was born to play.

Living a good and humble life he is the Man,
Having a dream come true with a good plan.
Graduating with God given talent from life's college
And walking up the ramp,
He was destined to be a Champ.

It Makes Sense to Get along

The ears say if you hear what I heard?
Then you wouldn't be a nerd.

The eyes are saying if you could see what I saw,
You wouldn't be chewing on that straw.

The nose is saying if you could inhale that smell,
You'd find someone to tell.

The hands are saying if only you could touch,
You wouldn't be sad as much.

The tongue is saying if only you could taste,
A lot of stuff you wouldn't waste.

The heart is saying what if I didn't keep up my beat,
You'd all be lifeless meat.

The head cries out Hey wait a minute, I'm the boss,
Without the brain you're all at a loss.

Okay everybody now it's time for me to step in,
The feet took you everywhere you've been.

We 're all working together for the same cause,
Put all the bickering on pause.

We all thrive and operate from the same vine,
Stop always claiming things as mine.

Looking out of my window

After rising each morning on my knees I'm praying,
Growing older my hair is graying.

The kids are off to school with smiles and waving byes,
While sleep loses the battle with my eyes.

I watch as a lone dog struts across a neighbor's lawn,
He marks his spot before dawn.

A bird is happily singing for the joy of an early spring,
I never know what daylight will bring.

When the sun comes up the children are walking to class,
I head to the kitchen to refill my glass.

Women begin to drive up, park and walk to the track,
Trying to get that girly figure back.

As the day shifts along at what seems a snail's pace,
A bird flying by glances at my face.

A police car on patrol spots a driver who didn't click-it,
Pulled the truck over and gave him a ticket.

Day by day objects anew, things and beings my eyes meet,
Enjoying life that is precious and sweet.

Get off my back(bull)

So, you want to ride my back,
You must be smoking crack.

Didn't you see what I did to Bob,
Find yourself another job.

You tied a rope around my belly,
I'm going to shake you like jelly.

The judges give you a time limit,
Don't climb on if you're timid.

You will spur me with your boot,
You won't be making any loot.

The crowd will scream and yell,
You'll have a sad story to tell.

You have an eight second count,
Sorry Bud you must dismount.

Before time you knew I would kick,
Now you're on the ground sick.

Tell the doctor it was just your luck,
Being cute you forgot to duck.

Remember to keep a room booked,
Next time you'll get hooked.

I came out and gave it my best,
Now it's time for me to rest.

Next year aloud my nostrils will blow,
I'll be performing another show.

The Fast Calf

Okay, you think you want to be a real cowboy,
You think it's something you'll enjoy.

Well, I guess you think that you can really rope,
I'm going to make you look like a dope.

This is one calf that dance to a different beat,
I'm the fastest calf you'll ever meet.

For you and your pony, today will be a big bust,
You'll both be eating a lot of dust.

I don't know why you keep coming around,
This is my old stomping ground.

I'm not going to let you put a rope around my neck,
When I'm done, you'll be a total wreck.

You come out to perform before a panel of men,
You'll never hear them say you win.

I'll never give you the opportunity to brag,
I'm too fast for you and your nag.

You need to feed that old pony more than just hay,
He couldn't catch me on my slowest day.

You can kick him, and you can beat him with a paddle,
You won't get close enough to leave the saddle.

Now if you're not careful you could get hurt,
Chasing me you'll eat a lot of dirt.

I hope you were smart and paid up your rent,
Off me you won't make a cent.

I noticed in your rope you have a crimp,
In your walk I'll put a limp.

Maybe one day you'll act like someone with sense,
Do like the rest and sit on the fence.

I don't know if it's you or that old hay burner,
One of you are a very slow learner.

Maybe you should go and try to catch a slow deer,
Come back and try it again next year.

Mockingbird Space

Let it be known to all the critters that roam,
This here is the spot that I call home.

Now as far as your little beady eyes can see,
All this territory belongs to me.

If you so much as think about invading my space,
I'll be all up in your face.

As for you Squirrel, I'll snatch the hair right off your tail,
Tell your friends you scratched it on a nail.

If that old noisy Blue Jay ever comes back my way,
I'll pluck his feathers, giving him a bad hair day.

To all those flying and walking that are smart and sane,
You better beware this is Mockingbird Lane.

There is another thing that you all should know,
I fly high and I fly low.

Now that old sneaky Tomcat is a little hard to beat,
I keep pecking him, but he always lands on his feet.

I rise early in the morning to dance and sing,
Giving praise to the Savior and King.

Well, it's time for me to fly around and check over the place,
Making sure there are no intruders invading my space.

Rooster the yard bird

I'm the meanest thing on the yard since chicken soup,
I'm the rooster that runs this coop.

When that old chicken hawk snatched feathers from my tail,
I didn't even flinch or yell.

Although I've aged and wearing something called lens,
I'm still the favorite of all the hens.

Because I'm a gifted Rooster, strong, fast and very wise,
I crow early alerting the farmer that it's time to rise.

As I flap my wings and began to yawn,
I see a dog stretching on the lawn.

The hens are preparing to lay some fresh breakfast eggs,
While the cows and horses are stretching their legs.

The sly fox is licking his wounds, heading back to its house,
He stepped in a trap that was set for the mouse.

For the quacking old duck today is not a winner,
It's been set aside for thanksgiving dinner.

Yesterday I had to give the young bulldog a taste of my spur,
I knocked a patch of hair from his fur.

Now that I got their undivided attention and they are all at a loss,
I can strut and flap my wings, because I am the Boss.

The Late Squirrel

I must rise early before the hunters get up,
There's no food in my cup.

One day I overslept and got out of bed late,
That's when I almost met my fate.

The hunter had brought a dog with him,
It was hard to shake them.

It didn't seem to matter wherever I'd go,
That dog always seemed to know.

I hopped and scampered from tree to tree,
That dog wouldn't let me be.

It didn't matter which way I went,
That old dog had my scent.

I tried using some of my grandpa's old tricks,
The hunter started throwing sticks.

He tried to make me come around to his side,
I was doing my best to hide.

I slowly stole my way up to the treetop,
Then I heard a loud pop.

The hunter was shooting and becoming a pest,
I wished I were home in my nest.

In the nook of a tree limb I curled up like a ball,
The hunter couldn't see me at all.

I learned a very valuable lesson that day,
Getting up late doesn't pay.

Puppy Love

At first the embraces used to be warm and snug,
Now it seems I can't even get a hug.
They don't come out to play with me anymore,
I sit watching as they pass the door.

With my tail wagging and my tongue hanging out,
They don't even know what it's all about.
If it weren't for the old man I wouldn't be fed,
In a week I'd probably be dead.

The woman keeps saying she's going to take me walking,
All she's doing is a lot of talking.
First chance I get I'm going to run away from home,
I'm going where the big dogs roam.

Another dog came into the yard late one night,
I ran because he was too big to fight.
I politely but hurriedly went into my house and hid,
I'm not ashamed of what I did.

Hey! That dog stood at least two to three feet tall,
I'm not even thinking about you all.
Look at me I'm the little dog that was born a runt,
All I could muster was a grunt.

Because I had sense enough to gallantly run away,
I'm in good health and living today.
I probably shouldn't tell about what some calls, cowardly acts,
One day I ran from three stray cats.

I was in front of my doghouse in a playful mood,
A tomcat and his felines came and ate my food.
I can imagine how this must have made me look,
By three cats my food was took.

That big bold tomcat growled at me and I ran into my house,
From now on just call me a mouse.
When I began barking at night, the people get mad,
It scares off burglars they should be glad.

Human beings are hard creatures to understand,
They don't mind barking out a command.
I guess their little puppy love for me has grown thin,
I keep begging, but they won't let me in.

Mall Tired Feet

It looks like she's going to make this a habit,
Running to the Mall like a silly rabbit.

Whenever she goes through those doors,
We'll be walking in a lot of stores.

I hate window shopping with a passion,
Checking stores for a certain fashion.

Goes to twenty stores before she's done,
Trying on shoes and buying none.

Her eyes are always bigger than her money,
At the register she's looking funny.

Listening to us she wouldn't be in this mess,
Causing us a lot of stress.

To her it may seem like we're just talking,
What would she do if we stopped walking?

I think that it's time for her to get a crutch,
She's stepped on us too much.

When we get home the toes will give her a bill,
All complaints go to the heel.

The Tree's Dilemma

What a lovely day it's going to be,
Here comes my friend to water me.

He drags behind a long green hose,
Brushing a bug off his nose.

Ah, Yes, yes, that really feels good,
He'd never use me for wood.

There are some things that I really hate,
He often forgets to close the gate.

A dog comes in and makes his mark,
Leaving it all over my bark.

My sap cries out hey you! Get away,
He doesn't hear a word I say.

I try to shake acorns down on his head,
A single leaf falls instead.

I don't mind if he comes by for shade,
His mark cuts me like a blade.

Day by day it's beginning to stick,
I need to do something quick.

While I stand here and quietly think,
My roots complain of the stink.

How I wish that I could run and hide,
Go out to sea on an early tide.

I am forgiving it's not too late,
Please remember to close the gate.

Mystery Woman

Men watch her as she sits and talks on her show,
Radiating the most sparkling glow.
Today seeing a woman like her is not very common,
She is considered a wise woman.

Men who don't have a woman in their life,
Would ask her to be their wife.
A man with a head full of hair with no curl,
He'd give her man a run for his girl.

She has been around the world and back,
Nothing on earth does she lack.
Traveling around to a near and far away city,
To the poor she shows pity.

Because she's a woman who's one in a million,
She deserves her own pavilion.
Her man shows her off on each coast,
About her he always boasts.

Some men's heart craves what cannot be,
She can only be for some to see.
There are other men who think like most do,
Secretly they're admiring her too.

Over the Internet love for her they would post,
For her love men strive to host.
If a Texas man misses a woman with his loop,
He'll pick her up with a swoop.

She is the therapy that gives her man's heart a lift,
Given by God as a special gift.
Dreamers being content watching her on TV,
Hearts knowing it'll never be.

Having a heart that's full of love, mercy and gold,
Hers is a story that should be told.
After everything is all said and the dealing is done,
For her man she's number one. {#1}

Balance of War

All through the scripture wars have been fought,
For battle young men are taught.
Every country will fight to protect its homeland,
Out on the sea and on the dessert sand.

Abraham, Moses and David all had to fight,
Standing up for something right.
Even when Joshua was in battle did God assist,
In the Bible you can find a list.

In most wars there will be some loss of life,
Making a widow out of a wife.
To protect the land and stay free there is a cost,
We all mourn for lives that are lost.

Fighting far away for home men are yearning,
While surrounded by ruins burning.
A boy goes off to war and comes back a man,
We must support them all we can.

Men will risk their lives for a friend and a stranger,
Removing the threat of any danger.
There was a place down in Texas called the Alamo,
A few men fought an overwhelming foe.

They all had the chance to run away and hide,
But instead they fought with pride.
Today we still remember the battle at the Alamo,
The men were not your average Joe.

Some wars were fought to set the captives free,
Just men couldn't let it be.
War never was or never will be a pretty site,
No holds are barred when men fight.

If our leaders didn't fight and for right make a stand,
We'd be prisoners in our own land.
If we get on one accord and pray to God for peace,
Maybe all the wars would cease.

Most people don't understand what it's all about,
Evil isn't going to cast itself out.
Before we go running around being a war hater,
Try living under an evil dictator.

Trouble Making Right Hand

Okay Righty don't do nothing stupid,
Like the time you played cupid.
You tried sliding down that lady's hip,
She busted the master's lip.

Remember when I told you not to fight,
I ended up getting cut that night.
You touched the hair of a man's wife,
He pulled out a carving knife.

Then there was the time at the Rodeo,
I told you to let's go.
On a policeman you spilled two drinks,
He put us both in iron cuff links.

Even that Friday night down at the bar,
You leaned on a man's car.
He twisted you like a soft piece of metal,
I had to wait for the dust to settle.

I can't count all the scrapes we've been in,
Starting fights, you couldn't win.
Now be aware that there will come a day,
I'll look the other way.

At first, I thought hanging with you was fun,
But now I must carry a gun.
Since I'm always pulling you out of the fire,
This left hand should be for hire.

"God is good all the time."

Made in the USA
Middletown, DE
18 March 2022